T0129699

God's Angels WALK AMONG Us

A BOOK OF HOPE AND ENCOURAGEMENT

Veronica Matthews

WESTBOW
PRESS®
A DIVISION OF THOMAS NELSON
& ZONDERVAN

WestBow Press books may be ordered through booksellers or by contacting:

WestBow Press
A Division of Thomas Nelson & Zondervan
1663 Liberty Drive
Bloomington, IN 47403
www.westbowpress.com
1 (866) 928-1240

All Scripture quotations are taken from The Holy Bible, New
International Version®, NIV® Copyright © 1973, 1978, 1984, 2011 by
Biblica, Inc.® Used by permission. All rights reserved worldwide.

ISBN: 978-1-9736-8741-2 (sc)
ISBN: 978-1-9736-8743-6 (hc)
ISBN: 978-1-9736-8742-9 (e)

Library of Congress Control Number: 2020904580

Print information available on the last page.

WestBow Press rev. date: 03/12/2020

This book is dedicated to God, God's angels,
my beloved mother and daughter, my family,
and my friends who are family.

CONTENTS

PREFACE

I decided to write *God's Angels Walk among Us* after my beloved mother passed away on August 3, 2016. She was there for me on the day I was born and throughout my life. And I had the privilege of holding her hand when she passed from this life to her eternal home in heaven. My purpose for writing *God's Angels Walk among Us* is to lead you to find comfort, have faith, and believe that God has a plan for all our lives. Jeremiah 29:11 reads, "For I know the plans I have for you,' declares the Lord, 'plans to prosper you and not to harm you, plans to give you hope and a future.'"

I want to share with you a poem I wrote after my mother passed away. In the poem, I mention Minnie, my beloved longhaired Chihuahua puppy who passed away shortly after my mother. She died of a genetic defect at the tender age of seven months. I look at her death in a different way now. Minnie came into my life at the perfect time. She had helped me get through my mother's death, and she was Taco's best friend. (Taco is my smooth-coat Chihuahua.) Minnie was a gift from God. We all belonged together during the short time she had on earth. If I had known the outcome, I still would have chosen her. She was my angel on earth, and now she is my angel in heaven. My mother loved Minnie very much. My dad said that if I hadn't bought her, he would have bought her for Mom. I had a strong feeling all along that Minnie was my mother's dog. They are happy and safe together in heaven, and one day I will see them again. What a happy day that will be.

A Believer's Heart

At the time between waking and sleep
Is when the past calls to me.
I can hear your voice and see your face
With loving memory.
Some nights I fall asleep
And we have a visit, you and I.
When I awake from vivid dreams
Into reality, I cry,
Not because you're hurting,
Not because you are not safe,
But because your absence
Makes my mind, heart, and soul ache.
I try to remember the good times
Like you once told me to.

Some days I struggle,
Not wanting to disappoint you.
I know one day we'll meet again.
It seems so long from now.
I practice living in the present
And enjoy my life somehow.
On the day my eyes will see your face—
What a day that will be.
We will spend our time together
For all eternity.
I love you, Mom and Minnie.
I know you're watching over me.
And every day,
in my heart and mind,
I carry you both with me.

CHAPTER 1

God's Angels Are Real

God's angels are real. There are many scriptures in the Bible about angels. These are my favorite:

> For he will command his angels concerning you to guard you in all your ways. (Psalm 91:11)

> Do not forget to entertain strangers, for by doing so some people have entertained angels without knowing it. (Hebrews 13:2)

> Are not all angels ministering spirits sent to serve those who will inherit salvation? (Hebrews 1:14)

> Praise the Lord, you his angels, you mighty ones who do his bidding, who obey his word. (Psalm 103:20)

> The angel of the Lord encamps around those who fear him, and he delivers them. (Psalm 34:7)

I believe God sends His angels to protect us from harm, to guide us when we need direction, and to minister to us when we have a broken heart and feel hopeless. I was saved by God's grace when I was a girl of sixteen. Each and every one of us can become saved and live with God for all of eternity. Salvation is the greatest gift from God that humans could ever receive. All that is needed is to say a prayer and to believe it. "I believe that Jesus Christ is the Son of God and that He died on the cross for my sins. I confess that I am a sinner. And I ask You, God, to please forgive me of all the sins that I have committed. I repent. I ask You to please come into my heart and into my life. And I accept You as my Lord and Savior. In Jesus's name, amen." If you have said this prayer and meant it, then you will go to heaven. It's a onetime prayer; say it and you are saved. You cannot lose your salvation.

We will always sin, no matter how hard we try not to, because we live in a fallen world. All we can do is the best that we can do and ask God to forgive us when we do sin. John

3:16 says, "For God so loved the world that he gave his one and only son, that whoever believes in him shall not perish but have eternal life." I had been reading this scripture for thirty-eight years until one day I fully understood what God's Word meant. The key word is *gave*. When I realized that I didn't have to do anything to earn God's love and His salvation, it was a profound revelation. It is not good works that get us into heaven. There is nothing we can do. It is what God does for us (if we ask) because He loves all of us very much. It doesn't matter what we have done; as long as we ask for forgiveness, we will receive it.

I have two more brief but important topics to touch on before moving on to chapter 2. I believe that all animals go to heaven. I will share two scriptures. Matthew 6:10 says, "On earth as it is in heaven." There are animals and pets we love on earth—as it is in heaven. So they will be with us in heaven. Revelation 19:11 says, "I saw heaven standing open and there before me was a white horse, whose rider is called Faithful and True. With justice he judges and makes war." God is coming back on a white horse. If there are horses in heaven, then surely all of God's creatures will be waiting for us there as well.

Finally, many people question why terrible things happen in this world. They also question God. In Genesis chapter 3, Adam and Eve sinned in the garden of Eden. There lies the answer. We live in a fallen world, a world of sin where people have free will. We can choose whether to do right or wrong.

We are also in a physical world with gravity and various weather conditions, and there can be accidents. Lastly, there are genetics that predispose humans to certain health issues and diseases.

CHAPTER 2

The Physical Angels of God

My first encounter with a physical angel was when I was nineteen years old. I was coming back home from an evening at a youth fellowship event at church. My friends and I stopped at a red traffic light, and we watched a horrific scene begin to unfold. The car behind us drove around us and ran the red light. Then the driver crashed into a vehicle that had the right-of-way. The other car spun uncontrollably across two lanes of traffic and into the woods. I leapt out of the back seat of my friend's car, and I ran across the road without looking either way. The woman's car had traveled deep into the woods, and the foliage hid it from plain view. She had slid from the driver's seat over to the passenger's seat, and she was shaking violently. I said, "You're all right. You're all right."

The woman began crying. She shouted, "The back of my head is bleeding! Can you look? Is my head bleeding?" She had broken pieces of shattered glass in her hair from the passenger's-side window, which was no longer there. I reassured her that she was not bleeding and that there was no blood as I held her hand tightly. She kept thanking me. I knew that she was fading in and out of consciousness. Instinctively, I knew I had to talk to her to keep her awake. While all this was occurring, I had felt a hand on my back, and I heard a male voice praying in another language. I felt the hot power of prayer go through his hand, through my body, and into the woman's body. I turned around and looked at the man. At first I was baffled because no one knew I was in the woods with this woman, not even my friends in the car. I looked into the man's eyes. They were the purest color of green I had ever seen. His eyes were filled with peace. I remember every detail of his face and appearance. I turned back to look at the woman, and I said to the man, "I wish I knew if she was going to be all right."

He replied, "She will be fine. She has a broken wrist and a sprained ankle."

I was startled by his response, so I turned to look at him. I was going to ask him, "How do you know?" But the man had literally disappeared! At that exact moment, the police entered the woods. I asked them, "Where did the man go?"

One policeman asked, "What man?"

I described the man in vivid detail. Another officer said, "Ma'am, there is no one in the woods except you. If there were someone else here, we would have seen him exit the woods." I was asked if I had been in the car accident and had injured my head. I said no. And I dropped the subject.

A huge crowd had gathered, and the police were busily asking questions. I answered all the officers' questions, and then I walked away and shook my head. Little did I know I would come across this very same angel again, thirty-five years later.

CHAPTER 3

The Invisible Angels of God

As a child, teen, and young adult, I had experienced many of God's angels. But they were not in human form. Unlike the physical angel in chapter 2, these angels were invisible to the eye, but I physically felt them. They physically touched me, and they had protected me from harm and also from death.

When I was eight years old, I was late for school one wintry morning. As I ran to school through snowdrifts eight feet high, my coat opened. I didn't stop to button it back up. My elementary school was one mile away. I didn't feel well during school that day, but I stayed until school was dismissed. Then I began my one-mile trek back to my house. Later that evening,

I furiously rocked back and forth in my rocking chair. My back hurt terribly, and I felt really ill. Something was really wrong. I told my mother, and she took me to the doctor. My diagnosis? I had double pneumonia. I was immediately hospitalized, and I stayed for three weeks.

I'm not sure how many days I was there before the fateful night occurred. But one evening I woke up and couldn't breathe at all. I bolted upright in my hospital bed after having been in a deep sleep. My eyes were like saucers. I tried desperately to inhale air. I panicked! I was frantically reaching around, trying to find the emergency button to call the doctor and nurses to help me. I fumbled until I found the button, and once I found it, I pressed it for as long as I could. Then I felt the button slip away from my hand. I hoped I had pushed it long enough for everyone to know that I needed help.

It seemed like an eternity before help arrived. Everything went black, and I thought to myself, *This is it. I'm going to die.* I heard God's angels praying for me, and I felt them all around me. Then I started to drift back into the earthly realm. I heard the doctors and nurses shouting. There was such a commotion. I just wanted them to know I was okay. I was coming back. I felt something over my face. It was an air mask. At first my eyes opened like slits. Then I was blinking. Initially my vision was blurred. Everyone shouted with joy that I was awake. I was fighting to take off the air mask because it pinched my nose and I couldn't breathe and get air. Finally the nurse was able to understand what I was trying to say. Then the staff brought in an oxygen tent, and I was able to breathe comfortably again.

CHAPTER 4

Jesus's Visit

When I was thirteen years old, I was picked on mercilessly in school. I was extremely depressed, and my mother had great concern for me. My mom didn't know what to do. So she prayed. She prayed that Jesus would be in my room with me. That's all she could do.

God answered her prayer. I was on my bed crying, and I saw Jesus slowly appear in the corner of my bedroom. He was standing there looking at me with such great love and peace in His eyes. I remember just staring at Him and wanting Him to stay with me for as long as possible. He stayed with me for a few minutes. Then He slowly vanished. I will never forget that as long as I live. God cared for me so much that He visited me.

My life was forever changed for the better that day. It didn't mean that all my troubles would be gone for the rest of my life, but it caused me to know that with God all things are possible. And there is nothing to fear with God. I have tears as I write this because God's love is so overwhelmingly pure and good.

CHAPTER 5

The Bull

Visiting my grandma's dairy farm in New York was the happiest time of my life. It was heaven on earth for me. It's where my love of animals was born and nurtured. Schoolkids could be mean, but the farm provided me with a place of solace, peace, happiness, and freedom. Animals are pure sources of unconditional love. They listened without judgment, and they were always there for me. The animals accepted me for who I was as a person. And I could be myself around them. I felt a sense of safety and security being among their kind. My compassion and love for all animals remains to this day. They have always been, and always will be, a big part of my life.

At school I was painfully shy, but around the animals I

was confident. I am surprised I have lived to tell the tales of my misadventures on that farm. I behaved recklessly, not only because I was a child, but also because I believed the animals would never hurt me. Anytime my cousins would dare me to try something dangerous, I would do it to prove to them that I could do anything. God's angels were working overtime to get me safely to adulthood.

On one visit, my grandma had just bought a new bull. She told me, and all the kids, to stay out of the bull's field. Grandma said he was aggressive and that he would chase and trample kids. After the lecture about the bull, my cousin and I left the farmhouse to play outside. Then my cousin dared me to enter the bull pasture. Foolishly I accepted with the condition that she would have to take her own dare as well. We both walked to the bull's pasture, and we squeezed through the barbed wire fence. From a distance, the bull looked small and not very intimidating while he was grazing on a patch of grass underneath a large tree. He had turned his massive body to look at the foolish children who had dared to enter his territory. My heart was pounding out of my chest, but I continued to walk closer to this impressive beast. My cousin and I had walked far into the field. I started to think that the bull wasn't aggressive at all and that I could actually go up to the bull and pet him on his face.

As if the bull had read my mind, he took a deep breath and bellowed loudly. It was ominous! Then he started digging at the ground and kicking up divots in a rage. My cousin yelled, "Run!" We raced back to the fence as fast as humanly possible. My cousin was older and taller, and she ran faster. I remember her hurdling the three-tiered barbed wire fence with ease. And she kept running! I was short, and I knew I couldn't follow suit, so I dropped to the ground and tried to crawl underneath the barbed wire. I crawled headfirst on my belly, but the back of my shirt kept snagging on the barbed wire. I was numb to the bits of metal ripping into my skin. I screamed for my cousin to help me. She ran back and lifted up the barbed wire closest to the ground. At that point, I had turned my body around. I inched my way out on my back, moving feet first! She was screaming, "Hurry! Hurry! He's almost at the fence!" Then she dropped the barbed wire and ran for help.

I prayed as I kept inching my way out at what seemed like an eternal snail's pace. I cut my hands on the barbed wire as I was pushing it away from my body and face. I heard and felt the bull's thundering hooves pounding the ground. He was coming closer and closer. His bellowing was even more furious, and it was getting louder. I was almost out! So close! Then I closed my eyes, fearing this was the end. That's when I heard it: a loud and thunderous thud! The bull forcefully exhaled like he had run into a solid wall. God's angel stopped the bull right before he had reached the fence! I was still lying on my back, shaking. I was exhausted and frozen with fear.

Since I wasn't in the midst of being trampled, I decided to open my eyes. As I blinked the sunlight out of my eyes, I saw that I was miraculously on the other side of that fence! The bull's head was leaning down over the barbed wire within a few inches of my face. He bellowed loudly and proceeded to slobber all over my face. But he just stood there, staring at me helplessly. It was as if he were temporarily frozen and immobile. Just then, a farmhand grabbed my ankles and dragged me away from the fence that the bull was still standing behind. In that exact instance, it was like the bull was released from the invisible barrier that had been holding him back. He went into a rage and dug up the earth and flung his head up high in protest. He pushed against the barbed wire in an attempt to break through it. But after a few tries, he reluctantly conceded. He turned, bellowed, and trotted off back to the spot where he grazed under a tree. The farmhand, and my cousin and I, never told my grandma what had happened. No one would have believed what we had experienced. We wouldn't have believed it either, but we had seen it with our own eyes.

CHAPTER 6

Diablo

I was enjoying an exceptionally beautiful day on my grandmother's farm. I rode a quarter horse through the golden wheat fields and felt the sun and wind upon my face. I could feel the wheat brushing against my blue jeans as my heart beat in rhythm with the pounding hooves of my steed. I heard the wind as it tickled my ears and blew through my long brown hair. The red-winged blackbirds were singing, and the Boston terriers were barking as they ran alongside me through the seemingly endless fields. Brownie's hoofbeats were steady and sure as we confidently loped onward. I remember the sound of the swishing wheat that surrounded us, and I remember the sweet fragrance of the wildflowers mingled with the wheat.

The weather was perfectly comfortable with the white fluffy clouds playfully making animal shapes against the contrast of the blue sky. The Bostons would flush the blackbirds out from their hiding spots, which made them look like kernels of popcorn flying up into the air. I closed my eyes so I could seal this moment in time and in my memory forever. I was happy, peaceful, and free.

I walked my horse to cool him down and then led him to his stall for a well-deserved rest. I patted the side of his beautiful dark brown neck and was thinking of what I would do next.

I decided to take a long and lazy walk among the Holstein cows in their grazing pasture. And I hoped to find a few deliciously sweet blackberries that might have been skimmed over on the bushes at the end of the field. I was completely lost in thought when I suddenly became aware of my surroundings. I had heard the tales of the infamous Diablo. She was so named because of the huge white horns on her head. She was the lead cow, which meant that she was the boss cow. She would protect her herd at any cost. My body responded in fear upon the impressive sight of this magnificent beast. She was a legend. I gulped air and started to sweat. I tried to talk myself down from the actual fear I was facing, which was standing just a few short yards in front of me. My mind was racing. Well, no time to think! She was running toward me at top speed! Instantly I turned and started running back to the barn, where I knew I could climb up the ladder to the hayloft and be out of harm's way.

I hadn't realized how far I had walked until I saw a tiny red speck in the distance. It was the barn! I knew Diablo could easily outrun me, and I thought how sad everyone would be when they found my trampled body alone in the pasture. Just then, I saw a ring of cows lying down to my left. I knew this was my only hope of survival. I ran even faster. I hurdled over the back of one of the cows, landing in the center of the cow circle. I completely startled the Holstein I had leapt over; she bellowed with surprise and stood up. Then the other cows followed suit.

As soon as my cow shield had stood, Diablo knocked into her side full force. I ducked down as Her Majesty stretched her neck over the back of my cow and strained to see where I had gone off to. She was bellowing angrily, smelling the air, and profusely slobbering. My cow made soft moos, which seemed to appease the enraged lead cow. It also seemed to somewhat pacify her. Diablo blew out a long sigh, though I could see she was baffled and was still searching for me. She would swing her head left and right. I didn't want to stand there all day, so I reached up to my shield cow's ear and I bent it gently down toward me. I whispered softly, "Caboss, caboss." This was how my grandpa called the cows from the pasture when it was time for them to be milked. Well, it worked! My cow mooed and started to slowly head back to the barn. Meanwhile, several Holsteins had surrounded me.

We all slowly started the extremely long journey back to the barn. All the while, Diablo was on the lookout for me. She was determined.

It seemed like three hours later, but we were almost at the back entrance of the barn. The whole time, I was trying to figure out how to escape Diablo. We would all have to enter through the narrow space and go into the barn together. Too late! We were there. Then I remembered that all the cows knew which stanchion belonged to them. The herd instinctively ran to their assigned places inside the barn, including Diablo. I ducked off to the side, behind the lead cow, and safely got to the ladder, where I climbed my way up. I sighed with relief and collapsed on a haystack. I thought about how I would explain to my grandfather why the cows were already in their stanchions to be milked. I got up and headed for the farmhouse while my grandfather headed toward the barn. We met halfway. He looked at the pasture of empty cows and looked at me. Then he said, "Thanks for calling the cows in for me." I smiled and continued on my way because I was late for supper.

I know God saved me from Diablo. It was as if the cows understood the situation and protected me by safely guiding me back to the barn. God sent His angels, once again, to protect me that day. I am truly grateful for my life.

CHAPTER 7

Wild Thing

Wild Thing was the latest dairy farm acquisition. He was a strange-looking pony with an odd-colored coat. I was informed that he was a Peelway pony. I had never seen one before, and I have never seen one since. Wild Thing's name should have tipped me off. He was a green broke pony, which means that he was still half wild and not completely tamed. Well, two of the foster kids dared me to ride Wild Thing with no saddle. His mane had been recently shaved, so there was literally nothing to hold onto. He was so wild, I'm not sure he even wore a halter. All I remember is hopping on his bare back and grabbing the rope that hung loosely around the base of his neck. The two foster kids were riding Brownie, the tame and steady quarter horse.

At first, all was well. Wild Thing just ambled along with me, and I was confidently riding on his back. I turned my head to the foster kids and said, "He's not so bad." As if Wild Thing understood what I had said, he suddenly pinned his ears back—and I was in for the ride of my life! The only way I can describe the experience is to liken it to bareback bronc riding, which I've seen at rodeos. Wild Thing threw his head down between his front legs and kicked his hind legs high toward the sky. I slid downward toward his neck as I was screaming at the top of my lungs. The only way I could balance myself was to put my left hand forward against the base of Wild Thing's neck and to put my right hand behind me on his lower back. That way, I could somehow slide back and forth between his wild bucking and rearing up on his hind legs.

All I could see were the rocks that surrounded me on the ground. They looked blurred from his wild rodeo moves. I knew I couldn't find a soft patch of grass to fall onto, so I continued my balancing act and held on tight. For a moment, I glanced over at the foster kids. They had both laughed so hard that they had fallen off Brownie and onto the ground. I thought I'd be joining them on the ground too, except my head was going to be cracked open on the rocks and I'd be trampled to death.

Well, I had a moment of clarity in between racing thoughts.

I remembered that when you pat a horse gently on the side of the neck, it is a reward for the horse's behaving well. And when one is trying to kill you, one solid punch to the side of the neck lets him know that you are the boss and that he needs to stop his bad behavior. The punch would not hurt the horse at all; it would just startle him into behaving, or so I thought. So I punched Wild Thing as he reared up on his hind legs. I shouted, "*Knock it off!*" He came back down and planted all four hooves firmly on the ground. He stood motionless for a moment. His ears were still pinned back. Then he swung his large horse head to the right and grabbed the leg of my blue jeans. He almost got a piece of my leg with it. Wild Thing was smart; he was trying to pull me off his back! As he was pulling, I looked him straight in the eye and pointed my finger toward his face. I said in a low and deep voice, "If you don't stop, I'm going to hit you so hard, I'll knock you into next week!" It was a cheap threat, but would he call my bluff? Well, it was a standoff. Wild Thing continued to stare for a moment with great intensity and with my jeans still in his teeth. I could tell he was thinking about what he was going to do next. Then he broke eye contact and dropped my pant leg. He blew out a long sigh of defeat. I was shocked! I had successfully tamed my first horse.

I sat proudly with a smug look on my face. The foster kids stood slack-jawed in the pasture, just staring at me and Wild Thing in disbelief. Then they got back on Brownie's back, and we all rode gently and easily back to the barn.

CHAPTER 8

The Stallion

I loved visiting my grandparents' dairy farm several times a year. It was a trip filled with great excitement and anticipation. There were always new animals added to the menagerie each year. This year, there was a magnificent shiny black stallion that was seventeen hands tall. He was a Thoroughbred racehorse! I was mesmerized by the most beautiful creature I had ever seen in my entire life. It is difficult to describe his raw beauty. His powerful muscles exuded a grace and strength that I had never witnessed in a horse before. I wanted to ride the stallion more than any of the other horses on the entire farm. My cousin gave me the obligatory warnings: One, he was a stallion, and therefore he was very dangerous.

Two, he was barn sour. A horse that has gone barn sour—which means that he has been kept in a barn too long—is an extremely reckless creature. In this case, the horse had been kept in a barn over an entire New York winter. Winters in New York are a minimum of nine months long. So every chance the horse got, he would run back to the barn, where he felt safe. It's similar to agoraphobia in people—the fear of leaving the house. With the stallion, it was fear of leaving the barn.

I was asked if I wanted to ride the Thoroughbred, and I answered by getting a leg up on top of him and getting myself comfortably seated on his bare back. I assure you it was a wow experience. Feeling the power of the horse's muscles was intoxicating. And looking down from his great height was euphoric. I gently squeezed his sides with my legs, and he loped around the ring like royalty. We loped three times around the ring before I noticed impending doom. One of the foster kids was opening the gate to come in and watch me ride the black stallion. Well, that's all it took. The horse saw his chance to escape to the barn, and I couldn't hold him back. The leather reins cut deeply into my hands. I was utterly helpless. At that moment, all I remembered was someone shouting, "Don't get in the stall with him! He will kill you!" I wish she had warned me before I took a ride on this majestic beast.

All the kids on the farm were running after me and the stallion. He was racing toward the barn at full speed. I heard one cousin shout, "Get Grandma! Get Grandma!" You knew it was serious if you had to get my Italian grandmother involved. This was a matter of life and death. Thankfully, I received another moment of clarity. I ducked my head as the stallion ran into the barn. I had one split second of an opportunity, and I took it. I leapt off the stallion's back. He was safe in his stall, and I was safe too. The commotion of scuffling gravel grew louder as my grandmother and all the kids got closer to the barn entrance. Then I heard my cousin scream, "The stallion's in the stall! He's killed her! He's killed her!"

Grandma and the others called out my name repeatedly. I answered, "I'm here!"

"Where? Where are you?" my grandmother shouted.

I replied again, "I'm up here!" Everyone was looking at eye level all around the barn until I said, "Look up!" And in slow motion, everyone collectively looked up at me. I was stuck like glue to the barn beam. Suddenly everyone broke out into a cacophony of laughter, including my grandmother.

CHAPTER 9

The Palomino

Unbelievably, I have never fallen off a horse in my entire life, despite the fearless and reckless behavior of my youth. The only time I was really scared was the year that brought a new palomino horse to the farm. I don't remember the horse's name, but I assure you, I remember the horse's energy. The only words to describe this sad creature are *pure wide-eyed fear*. I have never seen such a large and panic-stricken horse in all my years. And of course I accepted the challenge to ride him. It took thirty minutes for me to get on his back. I had ignored all the red flags once again. This horse was huge, powerful, and scary. I remember feeling a half ton of shivering, quivering nervousness beneath the saddle. His energy was palpable. I ran him around the ring only once. Then I asked for help to get off him, and I never rode him again. It was one of the most frightening experiences I've ever had. The palomino was consumed by fear, and I knew he was not safe to ride. Horses are prey animals whose first instinct is flight. If he had gotten startled by a bird or a dog, I may not have survived. That was an unforgettable ride. The thought of him still takes my breath away as I write this chapter.

CHAPTER 10

Misty Morn

When I wasn't on my grandmother's farm, I was at summer camp riding horses. I loved horses so much, I wanted to have one of my own. So my dad took me to ride a horse that was advertised in the local newspaper. Misty Morn was a gorgeous dapple gray horse, which was my favorite color. He hadn't been ridden all winter. I pushed back the memories of the barn-sour stallion I had once ridden. This time I wore riding gloves to prevent my hands from being cut from the leather reins. And I was right to wear them. Misty was strong and powerful, and he was really hard to hold back. He was a hunter horse. Hunters, which are also steeplechase horses, love to run and jump over fences. I was told that Misty never refused to jump. It wasn't until I got right up to the fence that I realized that this was a five-foot jump! Suddenly I felt a sick panic wash over me.

At summer camp, I had jumped horses over three-foot fences with the reins in my teeth and my hands behind my back, but this was ominous. I tried with all my might to turn Misty Morn away from the fence because I knew I couldn't jump it successfully. I had a gut feeling. But Misty was stronger than I was, and he knew it. He took advantage of his strength. Plus he was overpowered by his own instincts and love for jumping.

Here we go! I remember hoofbeats and then silence as we sailed over the fence. Time stood still for a moment. And then it happened. As he was landing, I felt my rear end lift out of the saddle and over my head. I knew this was it, the end. Miraculously, I felt a large hand on my forehead, and it pushed me back down into the saddle. We had made the landing, and I was stunned. I looked over at my dad and Misty's owners, and they had a shared look of sheer terror on their faces. Then the owners looked at each other and it was like they hadn't seen what had happened. We thanked them and left.

Dad and I were silent on the drive home. I don't think either of us believed what had transpired that day. Finally I broke the silence and said, "Did you see it?"

My dad said, "Yes."

CHAPTER 11

The Partially Visible Guardian Angel of God

My parents, and my brother and I, had just moved to a new neighborhood on the other side of town. One of our neighbors had an attack-trained Doberman pinscher that often ran loose. I found this out the hard way. I was walking my Belgian sheepdog mix around the circle at night, and he stopped in his tracks. The hair on the back of his neck stood straight up, and there was a guttural growl coming from deep within his throat. My heart sank to the pit of my stomach as I watched the scene unfold before me.

The attack-trained Doberman was loose. He was running at full speed and was headed straight for us. All I could see was a flash of gleaming white teeth underneath the streetlight. I reeled in my dog's leash and ran for the house. It didn't help that my dog was pulling me in the opposite direction. He was prepared to fight to protect me. We struggled all the way to the doorstep. I pushed my dog into the house. My first thought was of the Doberman getting inside my house as well.

I turned around just as the Doberman leaped onto the porch, and I slammed the door in his face. Once inside, I realized that my knuckles had scraped against the bricks of our townhouse while I was frantically trying to get inside. Four of the knuckles on my right hand had been opened down to the white cartilage and bone. I put ointment on them and wrapped my knuckles in a paper towel, taping the makeshift bandage together. My mom prayed for me, and I went to bed. The next morning, when I took the bandage off, my hand was completely healed!

I lived in complete and utter fear that summer. I started carrying a thin Wiffle bat with me whenever I walked my dog. I would never hit any animal with a bat. I just thought I could wave it in the air in a threatening manner and make the Doberman think twice about attacking us.

One afternoon I was walking my dog, and I had a bad feeling in my gut once again. I looked over and saw a different-colored Doberman running toward us at top speed! I started waving my bat in the air. I screamed with quavering fear, "I rebuke you in the name of Jesus!" The Doberman instantly stopped and ran back into the woods.

Later, I met the woman who owned this Doberman. He was a show dog. The woman befriended me and tried to ease my fear of the breed. I became so comfortable with her dog that I accepted her offer of a dog-sitting job.

When I went into the house, the Doberman was growling and barking at me. I ignored him and told him to stop it. Then something in my gut told me I was in big trouble. I hesitated, and fear completely enveloped me. The dog's pupils dilated, which meant that I was about to be attacked. Sure enough, the dog charged me. He pinned me against my only escape route, which was the front door. His paws weighed heavy on my shoulders as he stared menacingly down at me. He continued growling and was frothing at the mouth as slobber flew everywhere. The saying that one is frozen with fear is very real and accurate. I was literally paralyzed with fear. I could not move. My mind kept trying to figure out how to get out. I was so afraid, I couldn't even speak or call on the Lord in my mind for help. I thought this was the end. Then I saw a huge golden glow, the outline of my guardian angel, who appeared in front of me. The Doberman was then literally picked up into the air and was thrown halfway across the living room. The dog was frozen. He looked dazed and confused, but he remained still and quiet.

I knew I had to get out of the house, but my body wouldn't work. Then I was pushed through the front door. One second

I was on the inside of the house, and the next second I was standing outside on the porch facing the front door. The door was ajar. I tried to reach for the doorknob, but I was still temporarily paralyzed. Then the door slammed shut from inside the house. A few seconds later, I heard the Doberman barking, growling, and scratching at the other side of the door. I don't know how long I stood there. Time had stopped. Eventually I walked home and told my mom what had happened. Then I called the woman and told her that her dog had attacked me and I couldn't go back into her home. I didn't tell her anything more. She was shocked that her dog had attacked me.

After two Doberman attacks, I was afraid to go outside. I stayed in my house all summer and refused to walk my dog. One day, I decided I couldn't live like that anymore, so I prayed and asked God to take the fear of Dobermans away from me. Then I walked over to the house of the woman with the Doberman. I knocked on the door. She was shocked that I had come for a visit. I told her that I needed to get over my fear and asked her if I could come inside. She opened the door and grabbed her dog by the collar. I walked over to the couch. Fear was screaming out of every pore for me to get out of there. But I refused. I told the woman to let go of the dog, and she looked at me like I was crazy. "Are you sure?" she hesitantly asked.

I said, "Yes."

She released the Doberman, and he ran straight for me. We were eye level; he was huge, and the couch was low. I reached out and started petting him, and God took away my fear instantly. Then I kissed the Doberman all over his face while the woman looked on in disbelief. I might have gone overboard, but I wanted to be sure that my fear was gone.

CHAPTER 12

The Car Crash

There are many times in my life when I should have died. God has protected me and has saved me over and over again. I know I am supposed to be here for a purpose and a reason. Also, I know He has saved me from things I am not even aware of that have happened. You are here for a purpose and a reason too. I assure you of that.

My brother was driving us to the store, and I wasn't wearing my seat belt. There wasn't a seat belt law back then. The traffic light had just turned yellow, and it was raining outside. The roads were slick. My brother said, "I'm going to run it, or we'll slide into the middle of the intersection."

Unfortunately, the driver of the car facing us in the oncoming lane had decided he was going to run the yellow light as well.

My brother had continued through the light while the man was turning in front of us to go into the shopping center on our right. The sound of crunching, scraping, and scratching metal was deafening. We spun around several times. It was like a sick and twisted demolition dance. It seemed endless. Upon the initial impact, I knew I was going to fly through the windshield. I braced myself for it. Once again, God kept me in my seat. I didn't even feel my knees go into the bottom of the glove compartment until I saw the damaged car later.

When we finally stopped spinning, Mark asked if I was all right. I said, "Yes." Then he got out and ran to a phone booth to make a call and break the bad news to our parents. Immediately, people stopped and asked if we were okay. A security guard from the jewelry store ran up from the shopping center. He asked if we were all right. He said that he had never heard such a terrible accident in all his life. He said he knew that everyone would be dead. He could not believe we had survived. The car was totaled, and my brother and I had zero injuries—not even a scratch.

CHAPTER 13

The Legion of God's Angels

My family would take trips to Florida often, and we would fly instead of drive. My mom was an extremely nervous flyer. On one such occasion, there was a problem with the airplane. It was some sort of mechanical failure, and we were going down. We were thousands of feet in the sky, and everyone on the airplane was in a full-blown panic. The spirit of fear devoured and consumed everyone on that entire plane with the sole exception of my mother. My mom simply and calmly prayed. Then my mom and I heard the angels singing. She and I joined them in singing praises to God out loud. Suddenly the plane was all right, and we all made it safely to our destination.

CHAPTER 14

A Miracle on the Highway

When I was eight months pregnant, I visited my parents. They took me from our hometown, up the beltway, to a hospital for a routine gestational diabetes test. On the beltway, the driver of a giant vehicle was not looking where he was going, and his vehicle was coming into our lane. There were vehicles in front of us, behind us, and to the side of us. We were boxed in! My mom was screaming. My dad kept shouting that we were all going to die. I sat helplessly in the back seat waiting for the inevitable. My mom shouted to God to help us, and then a miracle happened. Everything went in slow motion. It was like being inside a protective bubble. The giant vehicle passed through our car and ended up to the right of us. Dad kept driving ahead. God had done something with time and space to save our lives. The three of us talked about that experience for years to come. God can do anything!

CHAPTER 15

Angels of Charity

When my daughter was a baby, we stopped for lunch at a local restaurant. When we were seated, I felt like someone was watching us. I looked out of the restaurant window and saw a veteran. He was standing on a median, in the middle of an intersection, staring at me. He was far away. I wondered how he could see me inside the restaurant. He looked directly into my eyes. I would look from time to time to see if he was still there. I felt that God impressed it upon my heart to give the man twenty dollars. I thought that he would be long gone by the time we had finished eating.

A little while later, I paid the bill and we left. To my surprise, the man was still there. And the timing of the traffic light was just perfect. I had a red light, and the veteran approached my car. He was scruffy-looking, but he had those peaceful, clear green eyes that I had seen only once before. I gave him twenty dollars, and he thanked me. I decided to give him another twenty-dollar bill, quickly grabbing it out of my purse before the light changed. In that split second, he disappeared. I looked in my rearview mirror and side mirrors, and I even craned my head out the window. There was no humanly possible way for someone to leave a scene so quickly. He would have had to cross many lanes of traffic. I know he was an angel and that he would give that twenty dollars to someone who needed the money, possibly a veteran.

CHAPTER 16

God Heals Animals

God not only loves and cares for us, but He also cares for our pets. When my daughter was five years old, our next-door neighbor had given her two goldfish. When I checked on them later, I was distressed to see that one had severely attacked the other. My daughter was worried too. I separated the fish, and we prayed for the little goldfish to be healed. I'm happy to report that the goldfish lived to be fifteen years old!

Currently my favorite Betta fish is named Sunny. I always felt sorry for those beautiful fish that were held captive in tiny dirty cups at pet stores. One cup of water was so murky, I couldn't see the fish inside it, so I decided to take him home. When I put him in his new and improved home, I found out that he is an extremely rare variety of Betta fish—a gold elephant ear half-moon. Yellow with large white pectoral fins, he is a sight to behold! I love his sweet and gentle personality.

Bettas are aggressive fish toward each other, and the males must be separated. They are also known as Siamese fighting fish. Sometimes Bettas will flare at their owners. Flaring is an aggressive posturing with gills forward while swimming back and forth. It means they are ready to fight. Sunny is a gentle spirit. He has never flared at me. One day, I had filled the water level too high in his tank, so I took a cup and put it down into the water to scoop some water out. When I came back from the sink, my fish was gone! I knew he was not in the cup of water I had thrown in the sink because I always checked.

I looked around on top of my desk, and then I kneeled down and almost stepped on a bug. Upon closer inspection, I saw it wasn't a bug; it was my beloved fish! The cup, when pressed down into the water, had pushed the water out and onto the floor. And it had pushed Sunny out with it. I gently scooped him up and put him back into his tank. I felt horrible about the accident, and I prayed for God to let him live. Sunny is still on my desk. I often look over at him as I type.

CHAPTER 17

An Angel in the City

I decided to attend a board game night with a gaming group on Halloween. I thought it would be a great opportunity to meet new people and make friends. I had a long drive ahead of me, and I had just purchased a navigation device for my vehicle. I typed in the address and then began my journey. Later, I discovered that the navigation device wasn't foolproof.

After an hour or so, I ended up somewhere in the local vicinity of where I was supposed to arrive. I saw a parking garage and decided to walk from there. When I walked up to the street level, I had to ask several people for directions. Despite confusing and conflicting explanations, I eventually found my way into an underground mall. I felt like a rat in a maze but without the benefit of a much-needed trail of cheese.

I had been walking around in circles for a very long time, so I asked for directions again. Forty-five minutes later, I arrived at my destination. It was a relief to see people seated at several tables. There was a flurry of people setting up board games and shuffling cards. It was eight o'clock at night, and I was surprised that I had arrived on time. New introductions were made as everyone played musical tables at the end of each game. I had so much fun, I lost track of time. It was 1:30 a.m.!

I asked several people if they would help me find my car, and not one person would help me. I even offered to pay twenty dollars for their time, but every last person refused. So I resigned myself to the fact that I would somehow have to find my way back through a maze of tunnels and over several blocks to reach my car. Things always seem scarier at night. The underground looked like a malevolent scene from every horror movie I had ever seen. There were times I walked alone and times I wished I were walking alone. There was one intersection where the subway exited. People were screaming and running, all of them dressed in frightening Halloween costumes. I found it unbelievable that I was in this situation as I continued walking in what I hoped was the right direction. All the shops were closed, and it gave the underground mall an eerie, postapocalyptic feeling.

After walking for fifteen minutes with sporadic bouts of

panicked running, I found myself behind a couple who were walking purposefully. I asked if they could help me find the street where the parking garage was located. They said, "We're exiting close to that area. Follow us! When we get on the street, we'll point you in the right direction." Whew! Thank God! I felt instant relief, and I was glad I had remembered to scribble down the street name where I had left my car. The couple were much taller than I was, and I'm five feet, five inches. Trying to keep up with their long strides had me at a jogging pace for the last thirty minutes of my journey. We finally got up to the street level. They pointed to the left and said, "The garage is that way." I thanked them and headed down the dark and isolated street.

I couldn't see the garage from where I was standing. It was about five blocks away. First, I needed to cross one street. I stepped one foot off the curb, and a car came careening around the corner out of nowhere. The person was driving at lightning-fast speed and almost hit me. The walk seemed even longer at that point, and the night seemed endless. I was in flight mode; every little noise I heard made me turn and twitch like a nervous little bird. I kept silently praying that God would help me get to my destination safely.

Finally I arrived at the garage building. I'd made it! With a long sigh of relief, I walked up the steps and reached up to open the door. I pulled the handle toward me, and it was locked! I felt my hope deflate into despair as I read the sign in the window: "The garage entrance is not accessible from the building at night." I started to feel panic well up inside of me. I didn't want to walk down into the garage from the car exit. I didn't know if there were people with ill intentions lurking around. This entire evening had been a complete nightmare. Just as I turned around, I saw a man riding a bicycle. I became afraid. I thought, *What is he doing riding his bike around at this time of night?* But he was the only person I had seen for a long time, and I really needed help. Yet I still wasn't sure if I should take the risk. I took a deep breath and called to the man before he got out of hearing range. He stopped and walked his bicycle over to me. I explained my situation, and he said he would be happy to help me. Before I could explain that the building was closed, he had trotted up the steps to the door. His back was turned to me, and I saw the sweetest sight my eyes had ever seen. The letters S-E-C-U-R-I-T-Y were emblazoned in neon yellow on his jacket! He said he had the keys to the building, but then he hesitated. He said he didn't want me to worry about being in a locked building with him. Then he asked if I would mind if he escorted me through the car exit of the parking garage. I said, "That would be fine." I was just glad that I could get to my car safely now. The man could tell I was nervous, so he engaged in idle chitchat. Soon we both noticed that I had become visibly relaxed. He walked to my right, on the street side, as we made our way down to the garage exit. He wanted to protect me from oncoming cars. It took us a long time to actually locate my vehicle. The underground garage labyrinth was as disorienting as the underground mall. I had never been so happy to see my car in all my life!

The guard made sure I was safely locked inside my car. He told me to wait there for a couple of minutes so he could ride his bike up the exit ramp. Then I could drive up and meet him at the exit, and he could point me in the right direction. I met him on the street level. He directed me to Main Street and said that I could find the highway from there. He gave me his phone number in case I got lost on the way home. I know this security guard was an angel sent from God to protect me and guide me safely home. I was alone on the street at night, when suddenly this "man" on a bike showed up when I was in dire need of help. It's miraculous that I didn't die that night although there were ample opportunities.

CHAPTER 18

International Angels

I received an invitation from a friend to visit South Korea. I had never traveled outside the United States. It was a once-in-a-lifetime opportunity, and I accepted the invitation. I drove to a travel agent to book my flights and choose my seats. I was a fearful flyer, and it was going to be a long trip, so I decided to use my savings to travel business class. The first flight was from the East Coast to California. Business class was booked, so the travel agent upgraded my seat to first class for the same price!

Before the first flight took off, I almost disembarked the plane and went home. My seatmate was rude and aggressive, and I felt uncomfortable traveling next to him. I left my seat and told the two flight attendants that I was going to have to get off the plane. Then I explained why. One attendant assured me that the plane was safe and that the pilots were very skilled. I told her that I wasn't worried about getting there safely; I was worried about being confined for a long period of time and not being able to get out. The other attendant said he was a life coach and told me that if I had a problem, he would talk with me and help me get through the flight. Then the female attendant asked if it would help if she could get someone to switch seats with me. I said, "Yes." So a very nice woman volunteered to give up her seat, and I thanked her.

Everyone had been so kind and accommodating. I was fine the entire trip, including two hours of very rough turbulence over a mountain range. When the plane landed, I smiled from ear to ear. My confidence had grown by leaps and bounds. I kept saying to myself, *I did it! I did it!* Although I knew God had helped me do it, I had never been prouder of myself in all my life.

I disembarked and speed-walked to my next connecting flight. The airport seemed like a huge city. My plane was on the opposite end of the terminal. At each airport, there was always someone there to guide me and help me to catch my next plane. There was a nice Korean man who helped point me in the right direction. And a pilot confirmed that I was heading in the right direction. The pilot asked me where I was going, and I said, "Incheon."

He replied, "I'm going to fly you there!" It made me smile.

Also, I was able to thank the woman who had switched seats with me. I told her that if it hadn't been for her, I would have gotten off the plane back in Virginia. She was very nice. We chatted for a bit. Then she gave me a book that she had just finished reading on the previous flight.

On the international flight, I thought about getting off the plane like I had on the domestic flight, but I thought about my friend who would be waiting for me in Korea. This time I had a great seatmate and I was very comfortable. The first flight, from Virginia to California, was five and a half hours. The flight across the Pacific Ocean would take twelve hours.

About nine hours into the trip, I was tired of being on the plane. My seatmate talked with me for the remainder of the flight. He showed me pictures of his family, and he had a lot of great stories to tell. The last three hours passed quickly. He was very nice. Also, he showed me where to pick up my luggage and where to meet my friend.

CHAPTER 19

Saint Benedict

On August 2, 2015, my mother was taken by ambulance to our local hospital. It caught me off guard because we had just celebrated her eighty-third birthday two days previously. My mom looked so pale and fragile lying there on the hospital gurney. She was dehydrated, weak, and tired. The doctors and nurses had to wake her up to perform a myriad of tests on her. I remember watching my mother's chest rise and fall. I was afraid she would stop breathing.

At one point the doctor entered the room with a solemn face. She said she was sorry to inform us that my mom had multiple myeloma cancer. At that moment, my entire life changed forever. My heart broke for Dad too. He loved my mother so much that he was in complete denial. The doctor's words didn't sink in. My mom was sent to one of the top hospitals in the country, and then she was sent to a rehabilitation center. After several months, my mother was finally able to come home.

I had often thought I had hit rock bottom in my life. But I was never even close before. I sank into a pit of hopelessness, and I couldn't bear it any longer. I started sobbing. I grabbed my keys, got into my car, and started driving. I was running away, but to where I did not know. Then I remembered my parents' neighbor who had told me about a Catholic church a few blocks away. I knew God would be there, and I wanted to run into His arms. The tears continued burning down my face and my vision was blurred as I tried to safely make it to the Catholic church. I pulled into the circular driveway, where I saw an older woman weeding around the base of a statue of Jesus. I got out of my car and ran to her in desperation. I was sobbing uncontrollably; she didn't understand anything I was saying. She asked, "Do you need to make a confession?"

I choked out the words, "No. I'm not Catholic."

She asked, "Do you need counseling?"

I said, "Yes." She hugged me, and then she walked arm and arm with me up the steps of the sanctuary.

Once we were inside, she pointed to a chair on my right. She said, "Please have a seat. A priest will be here shortly." I thanked her. I tried to gather myself emotionally, but to no avail. A short while later, a priest entered through the doors.

He looked like he had just stepped out of the pages of the Bible. He had the haircut of a monk and the long untrimmed beard of a holy priest. He wore a long black flowing robe. He turned his head in my direction and gently smiled. He welcomed me into the confessional room, but we were not separated by a wall. I talked with him, and his verbal responses were as if he knew everything I was feeling and everything about me. I thought God must have been telling him everything I needed to hear.

I went to my first Vigil Mass on the following Saturday evening. I was in the third row from the front, on the left side. When the priest came out, he spoke: "We are now joining worship that is already going on in heaven." As soon as he said that, the whole altar transformed. It looked like heaven and earth were one. Everything looked like it had turned to gold. God is described as light. Well, I was blinded by the white light of God's holy presence. From that moment on, I would continue to attend Mass because God was there.

I continued to have counseling with the priest, and he extended his compassion by visiting my dear mother on a regular basis. He had given us his mobile phone number; we could call him at any time and for any reason. My dad would always call me when the priest would visit them. I lived a few blocks up the street, and I would visit every time the priest went to see my mother. When the priest entered the room, God entered with him. There was unspeakable peace, and we all felt well in God's presence. The priest would listen to my mother's stories patiently and with great interest—even if she would tell the same stories over and over again because of the medication she was on. He would always stay for extended visits. He would pray for all of us. And it would give us renewed hope and courage to be able to continue moving forward despite the circumstances.

It was with a heavy heart that we learned that the priest would soon be going back to the monastery. He was called to a life of solitude. We were thankful God had brought him to us for the very time we needed him the most.

Honestly, I believed this priest was an angel of God—until the day I saw pictures of Saint Benedict. He had the exact eyes, nose, haircut, and untrimmed beard. Also, he would say many things that would lead me to believe that he was the actual Saint Benedict. God allowed him to come to earth for a time to help us.

When I went for prayer at the rectory, there was a low-flying airplane that shook the priest's house. He was quite confused and baffled. He asked me, "What is that?" I told him it was an airplane. He still looked confused. I found it surprising that he didn't know what an airplane was or what a plane sounded like. Another time my daughter went to visit him. I wanted her to meet him. She was speaking to him about something in the modern world. He asked her what she was talking about. She explained herself, and he seemed amused. Then he said that he didn't know about such things because he came from the Middle Ages. It made me pause.

And although he had a smartphone, he had much difficulty working it. There were other signs, such as the way he spoke and the vocabulary he used. He wrote in the same way he spoke. I realize that a priest from a monastery may not be familiar with newer technology, but I imagine one would be familiar with things of this century like aircraft.

CHAPTER 20

A Rental Car Angel

My parents had lived in Florida for many years, and they wanted to go back. It was as if Florida would magically bring amnesia to the past year and present circumstance. We had all agreed in what town to live before we left. The two-day drive was the easy part. My dad splurged and put us up in a fancy hotel for a couple of weeks while we were looking for rental homes. I noticed a car rental office in the main area of the hotel; I often passed it as I went to the hotel restaurant and to the gift shop. One morning, I felt compelled to ask the rental agent about the area. I told him where we had decided to move. He said that it was a nice location. Then he proceeded to tell me about the town where he lived. He elaborated on how young families were moving to that area, saying that it was the safest county in all of Florida. He suggested we look there. I thanked him, and then I went to my parents' hotel room and shared the information. My parents and I were in agreement that it would be better to look there. A local would know more about the area than we did. We didn't realize it at the time, but the rental car agent was one of God's angels. He led us to the exact area that we needed to be for my mother's future care.

Sometimes in life we must take an indirect route and go through a hardship that leads us to the correct path. This was the path on which we were about to embark.

We were pressed for time as we were down to the last few days of the hotel reservation. I found a seemingly idyllic rental home online. The moving company kept pressing my dad for an address and a move date, so we decided to put in an application for this house and start the rental process.

Most everything is done on the computer now, including renting a property. In a matter of hours, the lease was signed with all three of our electronic signatures. I had never met the agent in person. She left the keys under a potted plant on the front porch.

My parents had accumulated numerous boxes of items over the years. My mom's generation knew the hardships of war. Everything was saved, whether it was a strip of buttons cut from a worn shirt or various odds and ends that could be used later. My dad wanted to settle into the house right away.

It took him two weeks to unpack approximately one hundred boxes. One day, when he checked the mail, he received a coupon for a free air-conditioning inspection. He thought it was a good idea, so he called and got an appointment for the following day. The man arrived. He took his time, thoroughly inspecting the entire home from top to bottom. When he was finished, he said, "This house has toxic mold, and carbon monoxide is leaking into the home." We were shocked.

I contacted the rental agent, and she contacted the owner. They let us out of the lease so they could fix the problems. My dad spent the next two weeks packing up the entire household. I prayed about where we should move next. I had remembered a coffee shop that we passed along the way. I took my Bible and was determined to stay there until God gave me an answer. I had done this once before when I did not know what to do.

I had a one-eyed cat that had grand mal seizures. The seizures were so violent, she would run headfirst into walls. It was horrifying to watch. She had done this twice within a short period of time. She was in a lot of pain after each seizure because of severe muscle contractions. She would sleep for a long time afterward to recover from each episode. That was the first time I took my Bible to a coffee shop. I told God that I would not leave until He gave me an answer about what to do about the cat. I was considering having her humanely euthanized. My statement to God was not a threat; it was a declaration of faith. Matthew 7:7 reads: "Seek and ye shall find." I was seeking God's wisdom to find an answer. As I read the Bible, God spoke to me. He told me to go home and pray for my cat and ask Him to heal her. So that's what I did. She never had another seizure again.

I found myself seated at the coffee shop in Florida, Bible in hand. I sat there sipping coffee and wondering what on earth I would do. Then I looked out the window and saw a brand-new apartment complex. I knew this was my answer! Immediately I drove back to the rental house and told my dad to stop packing and come with me. Arriving at the rental office at 5:00 p.m., we signed the lease and returned with the deposit from the bank before they closed at 6:00 p.m.! This is where God wanted us to be. We had to go through the process of the rental house experience because we had never planned on moving to an apartment. We'd only thought to move to an apartment afterward because we knew everything had to be up to code.

I moved into the apartment while my dad was tying up loose ends at the rental house. I am a minimalist; everything I owned fit into my crossover vehicle. I unpacked within a couple of hours, and my little Chihuahua and I made ourselves at home. I continued helping my parents until they were settled in. I had kept in touch with the priest back in Maryland via phone calls throughout the duration of our move. When the time came that Dad and I needed help caring for my mother, the priest gave me the name of an in-home hospice.

CHAPTER 21

Hospice Angels

There came a point where my father and I could no longer physically care for my mother. Once again, I called upon the faithful priest who had helped us many times over the span of the past year. He gave me the name of an in-home hospice. I had called the hospice, and they immediately sent a staff member over to our apartment. Within a few short hours, a hospital bed and an oxygen machine were delivered. And appointments were set up with various staff members, a doctor, nurses, and a pastor. My dad and I truly believe that many of the nurses who cared for my mother (and my father and me) were God's ministering angels. We also knew there were many kind people who tended to all our needs. I always knew when an angel came on duty. When the day and night nurses called before their shifts, a phone number would come up on my mobile phone screen. When an angel called, "The phone call is coming from an unknown source" would appear on my cell phone screen. I am familiar with private numbers that show up as an unknown number, but I had never received a call from an unknown *source* before.

For the next week, angels and people would caringly and lovingly tend to my mother. Despite the physical pain my mother was managing, she never gave up her faith in God. She would always pray and always thank God. God gave her strength. God gave all of us strength. We prayed that my mother would be with us for her eighty-fourth birthday and for her fifty-seventh wedding anniversary. God sustained her for both celebrations.

One day the Holy Spirit impressed upon me to call my brother and have him visit our mom. He caught a flight out, and we had a great visit together. My mother was still talking, and she had a huge smile because she was surrounded by her family. My brother stayed the weekend and had to be back to work on Monday. After he left, my mom began to become more inward. She tried to speak to me, and I believed I understood what she was saying. Shortly after, she was unable to speak at all. I could tell she was spending time inside herself. She and God were working things out together. She was connecting more with the spiritual world rather than the physical world, where my father and I remained. God had orchestrated the timing of everything perfectly.

The morning nurse had arrived. She was an angel from God. I sat with her in my mother's bedroom. The angel asked me about my life, and I told her about all of it. I told her that I would be okay and my father would be okay. I know my mother heard every word because the angel said, "It's time." I asked her to get my father. I held my mother's hand as she peacefully transitioned from this life to her heavenly home.

CHAPTER 22

A Message in the Clouds

When my mother was a little girl, her nonna grandma passed away while Mom was at school. They were very close. My great-grandmother would call my mother "bellissima Sofia," which means "beautiful Sofia" in Italian. My mother was very upset and confused about her nonna's passing. She told God, "I don't understand. Can you please show me my nonna so I know she is all right?" At that moment, my mother looked up to the sky. In the clouds, she saw a beautiful horse-drawn carriage, and inside the carriage was her nonna. Nonna looked down out of the carriage window and waved to little Sofia. My mother waved back to her nonna, and she had peace. She thanked God and knew her nonna was all right.

After my mother passed, I walked outside and sat on the apartment stairs. I looked up into the sky. I saw a circular swirling of clouds. It was like a portal or a vortex. Then I saw my mother's beautiful face in the clouds. She looked exactly like in her wedding picture that was sitting on the shelf in the living room. I thanked God for showing me my mother one more time, and I knew she was all right.

CHAPTER 23

Leo

One of my mom's registered nurses was named Leo. He saw my statue of Saint Benedict that the priest back in Maryland had blessed. Leo asked, "Who is he?"

I said, "Saint Benedict."

He replied, "I know him. We go way back together." Leo looked very familiar to me.

When I looked into his eyes, I knew he was the angel I had seen before when I was a younger woman. He was the angel who prayed for the woman in the car accident mentioned in chapter 2. I believe he is Daniel from the Bible and that Saint Benedict knew him.

One night I was tired, but I did not want to leave my

mother's side. I was afraid she would pass away while I slept. I expressed my concern to Leo. He told me that Mom would be all right that night and that she would sleep peacefully. And she did. I was able to sleep that night too. It was the same blessed assurance that he had given me regarding the woman in the car accident.

Sometimes at night, after I'd had a difficult day, I would awake. When I opened my eyes, there would be an angel kneeling near my face. The angel would have his head bowed in prayer. He only came when I needed it the most. My Chihuahuas, Taco and Minnie, would also see him; they would silently watch him. Eventually my dogs got used to the angel and continued sleeping through his visits.

I spoke at my mom's memorial service. This is what I said: "I am convinced, from experience, that God sends angels and saints from heaven to help us on earth. They live among us and are dispatched at the perfect time to minister to our needs. I'm speaking literally, not figuratively. I believe the church back in Maryland is an angelic portal to heaven, as is the hospice in Florida. Every single angel takes care of Mom and me and my dad. Dad and I had met with another angel. I can't explain the miraculous lift of my spirit after she had left. And Mom's newest prescription was suddenly and instantly filled. As I sat in the car while Dad went into the pharmacy, I looked around with new eyes. I could see God's love and mercy. And for the first time in my life, I know that no matter what happens in my life, everything will be okay. God loves us very much. He has good plans for all of us. I can't explain it. I just know and feel it. God sends humans into our lives at the right time as well. So what should I worry about? Nothing! Sometimes we get caught up in our circumstances and we can't see. When we get caught up in God, we can see beyond. God has no limitations. He thinks outside the box. He can do anything. God is love."

CHAPTER 24

Gary

I have lost many family members, friends, and pets. It is a heartbreaking loss of ten loved ones altogether. As I mentioned at the end of chapter 17, God helps us, but we must also be willing to do our part. I had isolated myself and was in a self-imposed prison of complicated grief. God sends his angels to comfort His people. Despite feeling hopeless, I forced myself to get out of the house and go to the local coffee shop. I decided to eat outside on the patio. The weather was beautiful and comforting. An older gentleman came outside and asked if he could sit with me. I nodded, and he joined me for lunch. I don't know why, but I poured out my entire life story to Gary. He was compassionate and kind. He listened and genuinely cared. He shared many stories about God. He gave me scriptures to read, and they were just what I needed. He encouraged me. Gary invited me to a church in a nearby town, and I thanked him. Then he told me that he came to this particular coffee shop every weekday in the afternoons, adding that if I ever needed to talk, I could look for him and have lunch with him.

I was in a loop, repeating the same cycle. I'd retreat back into my life of solitude and then go to the coffee shop and look for Gary. I went many times when he wasn't there. But when I was at my lowest points, I would always find him, and he would eagerly tell me all that he knew about God. Each time I saw Gary, he would patiently tell me about the church and invite me to go. This was God telling me over and over that I needed to go to that church! I knew I should go, but I couldn't muster the strength.

Previously I had tried to be social and had gone to local hobby groups that I found online. I never felt like I was a part of any of the book clubs or women's clubs I attended.

One night, I felt God had impressed it upon my heart to visit my dad. The feeling wouldn't go away until I went. I passed by Gary's church on the way to my dad's. The sign said two simple words: "Letting Go." After sixteen months of wearing a cloak of complicated grief over the loss of my mother, I decided I couldn't live like that anymore. And I knew my mom wouldn't want me to. I decided to honor my mother by remembering her with joy and not sadness—and by not isolating myself any further and to be with God's people again. So the following day I went to church. I enjoyed the familiar Christmas hymns, and the sermon was exactly what I needed to hear. I took notes and I put into practice what I had learned. I know God will continue to heal me, and I know I have a purpose there. It is important to have the fellowship and support of a church. The people become your extended family. People aren't perfect; we need to always have a forgiving heart. We are designed to be part of the body of Christ. We are here to help others. This is our purpose in life.

CHAPTER 25

The Angel Vet Tech

I was online one day looking at pictures of Chihuahua puppies for sale. It was the same website from which I had bought Minnie four years earlier. I felt like there was a missing piece because of Minnie's absence. I realize she could never be replaced, but I hoped for a companion for myself and for Taco. I remember what joy we had with having two companion dogs. I scrolled through photos, and a tiny blue brindle and white puppy came up. I looked into her eyes and instantly knew she was the one. If eyes are the windows to the soul, then I figured she was a sweet soul like my Taco. I named her Brandy. She was too young to fly up from Florida, so we patiently waited for three weeks for her arrival. I was disappointed when I heard that her flight had been canceled. It turned out that it was too hot for her to fly to my local airport. Sam, the Chihuahua breeder, volunteered to drive her straight to my house. What an unexpected blessing!

When Sam arrived, he took Brandy out of her crate and handed her to me. At nine weeks she was tiny! She was not much larger than a hamster. I'd love to say everything went smoothly for the first few days, but I had to take her to the emergency vet twice within her first three days with us.

On the first visit she needed to be treated for diarrhea. I don't know what previous emergencies the veterinarian and staff had encountered before our visit, but they appeared harried and stressed. I had brought in a fecal sample. It turned out that Brandy had the parasite giardia, which is caused by drinking contaminated water. She was put on antibiotics, a dewormer, and subcutaneous fluids. They also tested her for parvo, and she was negative, so all was well.

The next day, Brandy crawled underneath my recliner; she couldn't find her way out, and she panicked. Immediately I used herculean strength to pull the chair off her. I thought maybe she was just afraid, so I kept an eye on her. While she slept, I moved the recliner outside to the screened-in front porch. When she awoke from her nap, Brandy turned her neck and screamed. So it was off to the emergency vet again.

You can imagine my anxiety, especially after having been there two nights before. This time, there was a new veterinarian and new staff. I was visibly shaken as I paced and cried. There was a vet technician standing in the background. He was watching me quietly while the receptionist checked us in. There was something peaceful about his presence. He came around to escort us back to the room. When I got closer I saw those familiar clear green eyes that I have seen from previous angels. God's peace was radiating out from him. My body instantly calmed down. My racing heart slowed to a normal rate, and my breath went from rapid breathing from my chest to slow, relaxed breathing from my abdomen. I felt God's peace, which passes all understanding.

The vet tech looked directly into my eyes and said, "She will be fine." And I knew she would be. The angel veterinarian technician took down all the information about the incident. Then he took Brandy back to the veterinarian for an examination. The veterinarian brought her back to the exam room shortly afterward. She said that Brandy was fine and that in her panic she bruised herself and may have a pulled muscle. Furthermore, she was too young for pain medication. So all she needed was rest. The angel vet technician was right!

I believe the receptionist and veterinarian were also God's angels. I have been going to that veterinary practice for years, and I had never seen that staff before. The next day, Brandy had recovered 100 percent! She's happy and healthy and is growing like a weed.

CHAPTER 26

The Angel in the Grocery Store

I must preface this chapter by stating that I have been dealing with borderline high blood pressure for quite a while now. I was in denial about having gained weight to the point where it was affecting my health. I had gained ten pounds a year for three years after my mother died. I was having headaches and blurred vision. I went to the doctor for another reason: I had an infected hangnail of all things. When she told me that I would have to be put on blood pressure medication very soon, reality hit me in the face. I left the office and immediately went on a healthy diet.

Losing weight and changing to a healthy lifestyle for the rest of your life is neither easy nor fun. It's human nature to want to be able to eat what you want, when you want, and however much you want. Motivation is fickle. What I have learned is that if you stick to a plan, you will get results. I don't know why I was surprised to learn that statement is true. It's not a matter of how you feel. It's a matter of persistence and perseverance. You can achieve any goal if you stick to it. Also, I kept trying to do it all on my own. Then I realized I couldn't and that I needed God. So I asked Him to help me, and now I am no longer struggling. I am resting in God. It's so much easier if you just ask God for help.

Losing weight is a slow process. There are no immediate results. There is no instant gratification or quick fix. Patience is key. I plateaued for one month before I lost another pound. I told myself that the weight would continue to come off, reminding myself that regardless of how long it takes, I should just stick to the plan. When I got discouraged, God would encourage me. The main thing is that I didn't give up. I kept going even if the results were slow. After the one-month plateau, God sent an angel to help me on my weight loss journey.

I was in the dairy aisle in the grocery store, and a man appeared out of nowhere. He approached me and struck up a conversation. He said he had high blood pressure, and he proceeded to give me advice on how to manage it. He said, "We're going to make it!" I left the store feeling uplifted and encouraged. The very next day, I got on the scale and found I had lost one more pound!

I'm taking life one day at a time and also one pound at

a time. I focus on other things besides food. And I enjoy my hobbies such as knitting. It gets rid of excess energy and keeps my hands busy. It's very relaxing, and it's a good way to get rid of any stress. It's important to find things you like to do. When you replace eating with hobbies you love, it really helps the process. If you make mistakes, forget about it and get back on track. It got easier over time because my taste began to change. I used to comfort myself with food. After back-to-back emergencies with Brandy, I really wanted to eat junk food, but I thought about it and then made the choice to stick to my healthy eating plan. That was a milestone. That was my turning point. If I could resist emotional eating, then I knew it would get easier after that. And it did.

It's unrealistic to say that I'll never have a cookie for the rest of my life, or a little ice cream. The difference is that I eat that one cookie or small treat and continue on my healthy eating plan. Success is continuing forward on your plan and not going back to old eating habits. Every day I do the best I can. I try to limit an unhealthy treat to once every two weeks and then continue my plan. It works. I reward myself with nonfood items for every five pounds that I lose. And I rewarded myself for that one stubborn pound that took me one month to lose.

I read labels. If a food is too high in salt, sugar, or fat, I pass on it. I take high blood pressure seriously. I don't want to be on medication for the rest of my life. If high blood pressure goes untreated, it can affect the liver and kidneys.

CHAPTER 27

Abuse

I feel like God wants me to share one more part of my life. I initially left this subject out because it's unspeakable. But it's important to tell my story to let others know that they are not alone and they are not the only one it's happening to. I will not go into great detail, but I will say important truths that may help those who have been in a similar situation.

The truth will always come out, and the truth will always set us free. I was abused by a relative when I was a child. Sometimes a person's death will result in the revelation of a deep, dark family secret. Upon hearing this news about what had happened, I found it to be very confusing and upsetting. And it made me angry. More accurately, I was enraged. My initial reaction was, *What am I supposed to do with this information as an adult?*

The mind protects us, but the subconscious spends a lifetime trying to reveal the truth. In one way it was a relief. My whole life finally made sense, all the decisions I had ever made, all my behaviors and reactions to the world and to the people in it. In another way, it was a mess to process it all. The good news is that God is our Father, Physician, Therapist, and Healer all in one. I am thankful to be alive, and I am thankful for my life. More good news is that what had changed me as a child didn't require that I remain that same way as an adult. I understood myself and began to grow in self-love and self-compassion. I started having forgiveness toward myself and others.

The subject of abuse makes most people extremely uncomfortable. And it can make people angry, even toward the person who was abused. This is because it's a reminder of what happened. Forgiveness and love are the answers. It's okay if you can't forgive right away or if you feel you can never forgive. I understand; I've been there. Forgiveness isn't for the other person. It's for you. When you forgive, you are not saying that what the person did to you is okay. You are doing it so the abuse does not have control over you for the rest of your life. I'd rather live a life of love and forgiveness than a life of bitterness and anger. It's not easy. And it's a process. But with God's help it can be done. All we have to do is choose it.

Every time the fact of my abuse comes back to mind, I make my thoughts captive to God and turn my thoughts over to Him. In Him we will find rest. As Matthew 11:28 reads, "Come to me, all you who are weary and burdened, and I will give you rest."

CHAPTER 28

The Role of Caregiver

A lot of times when a loved one is in hospice, family members can get angry with each other or downright irate. This has absolutely nothing to do with the person who is not well or with the family members. The person in hospice may be angry about losing his or her independence. Family members may be angry at the disease. Unfortunately, in everyone's frustration, anger and rage might emerge. People grieve in different ways—sometimes in crazy and angry ways. I've personally experienced this after the loss of not only my mother but also of another family member I'd had a close relationship with. I prayed and forgave. I thought the relationship would never be mended. However, over time, God healed and restored the relationship, and it grew even stronger. Matthew 19:26 reads, "Jesus looked at them and said, 'With man this is impossible, but with God all things are possible.'"

I pray for everyone who reads *God's Angels Walk among Us* that God will touch you in a special way and give you hope. Philippians 4:7 reads, "And the peace of God, which transcends all understanding, will guard your hearts and your minds in Christ Jesus." Amen.

Printed in the United States
By Bookmasters